SANJEEV KAPOOR'S

Desi Sabziyan

In association with Alyona Kapoor

www.popularprakashan.com

Published by
POPULAR PRAKASHAN PVT. LTD.
301, Mahalaxmi Chambers
22, Bhulabhai Desai Road
Mumbai - 400026
for KHANA KHAZANA PUBLICATIONS PVT. LTD.

© 2009 Sanjeev Kapoor
First Published 2009
Second Reprint March 2011

WORLD RIGHTS RESERVED. The contents - all recipes, photographs and drawings are original and copyrighted. No portion of this book shall be reproduced, stored in a retrieval system or transmitted by any means, electronic, mechanical, photocopying, recording or otherwise, without the written permission of the author and the publisher.

(4315)
ISBN: 978-81-7991-567-7

PRINTED IN INDIA
by Trident Offset Works
B-97/4, Naraina Industrial Area
Phase I, New Delhi

Author's Note

Desi Sabziyan

Here is a collection of recipes from across the country that celebrates vegetables the Indian way – sprinkled with spices and lightly anointed with oils. There is something in here for your every mood – intriguing Amrud ki Sabzi, spicy Mirchi ka Salan, aromatic Dahi Baingan and Shahi Dhingri Matar Paneer in an opulent gravy; elaborately prepared Dhaabe ki Sabziyan; a robust Wadian Aloo, followed by a creamy Malai Makai Palak. And if that were not enough to whet your appetite, remember what your mother always said: eat up those vegetables – they are good for you!

Here are some tips for getting the most out of vegetables:

- Wash vegetables well under running water before cooking to remove any traces of insecticide. This is especially true of spinach which grows closer to the ground and has mud clinging to its leaves.

- Scrape off or peel as little of the vegetables as possible as most of the minerals and vitamins are found just under the outer skin.

- Cut vegetables into large pieces to minimise nutrient loss. Soak cabbage and cauliflower in plenty of cold salted water to remove any insects that may be hidden between the leaves or florets. A couple of tablespoons of milk added to cauliflower while cooking will help retain its whiteness.

- To freshen up shrivelled vegetables, immerse in cold water, to which a few drops of lemon juice have been added, for about one hour. Overcooking vegetables destroys their texture and the important nutrients they contain.

- Do not add soda bicarbonate to retain the colour of green vegetables while cooking.

Happy Cooking!

Contents

Desi Sabziyan

Undhiyo	6
Amrut Ras ke Koftey	9
Amrud ki Sabzi	11
Aloo Posto	12
Aluchi Patal Bhaji	14
Bataani Kaal Curry	16
Bharwan Karele	18
Capsicum Kayras	21
Batata nu Shaak	23
Pyaaz ki Tarkari	24
Chorchori	26
Khoya Matar	28
Mirchi ka Salan	29
Batata Song	32
Gobhi Mussallam	33
Guar ki Sabzi	35
Bhindi Coconut Masala	36
Tameta Ganthia nu Shaak	38
Kachchi Makai Dhingri	40
Ker Sangri	42
Methi Papad ki Sabzi	45
Tender Coconut and Cashew Nut Sukke	47
Mixed Vegetables in Coconut Milk	50
Nadir Yakhni	52
Sai Bhaji	54

Palak Chaman	57
Sweet and Sour Tomatoes	59
Urulai Chettinadu	60
Dhaabe ki Sabziyan	62
Vegetable Ishtew	65
Shahi Dhingri Matar Paneer	68
Ennai Kathrikai	70
Tawa Vegetables	73
Wadian Aloo	75
Manje Kael	78
Sarson ka Saag	80
Chane aur Kathal ki Sabzi	83
Kaalan	85
Dahi Baingan	88
Arbi ka Khatta Salan	89
Malai Makai Palak	92
Khatta Meetha Kaddu	94
Simla Mirch Besan ke Saath	95

Undhiyo

Desi Sabziyan

Ingredients

6-8 small potatoes, peeled and chopped
100 grams yam (*kand*), peeled and chopped
2 unripe bananas, peeled and chopped
3-4 small brinjals, slit in four
25-30 broad beans (*papdi*), cut into 1-inch pieces
6-8 garlic cloves
4 green chillies
2 one-inch pieces ginger
1 cup chopped fresh coriander leaves
5 tablespoons oil
A pinch of asafoetida (*hing*)
1 teaspoon mustard seeds
Salt to taste
1 teaspoon turmeric powder
Grated fresh coconut, to garnish

Muthiyas
¼ cup gram flour (*besan*)
½ inch ginger
Salt to taste
½ cup fenugreek leaves (*methi*)
1 or 2 green chillies
Oil for deep-frying

Desi Sabziyan

1. Grind garlic, green chillies and ginger to a paste. Mix the chopped coriander into the paste.

2. Mix together all the ingredients for the *muthia* except the oil, and make a stiff dough with a little water. Divide into small portions and shape each portion into one-inch long, half-inch thick rolls. Deep-fry the rolls in hot oil, till golden brown. Drain on absorbent paper.

3. Heat oil in a thick-bottomed *handi*; add asafoetida and mustard seeds. When the mustard seeds begin to splutter, add the ground paste and the broad beans.

4. Place the rest of the vegetables in layers one on top of the other, interspersed with *masala* and broad beans. Sprinkle with salt and turmeric powder. Cook for five minutes over high heat.

5. Pour in one cup of water, cover and simmer over very low heat for ten to fifteen minutes.

6. Add fried *muthiyas* and continue to simmer for fifteen minutes. Shake the pan occasionally to mix the vegetables, but do not use a spoon to stir. Serve hot, garnished with grated coconut.

Amrut Ras Ke Koftey

Desi Sabziyan

Ingredients

¼ cup *khoya/mawa*, crumbled
½ cup gram flour (*besan*)
½ cup mashed potato
⅛ cup drained yogurt
Salt to taste
1 teaspoon red chilli powder
2 tablespoons raisins (*kishmish*)
2 tablespoons broken cashew nuts
4 tablespoons fresh coriander leaves, chopped
4 tablespoons oil + for deep-frying
1 cup ground *masala*
¾ cup thick yogurt
1 teaspoon sugar

Masala
2 medium onions, chopped
1 inch ginger, chopped
8-10 garlic cloves, chopped
2 teaspoons coriander powder
½ cup grated fresh coconut
½ teaspoon turmeric powder
1 teaspoon red chilli powder

Desi Sabziyan

1. Roast *khoya* on a *tawa* till golden. Add *besan* and continue to roast for a while. Transfer the mixture to a bowl.

2. Add potatoes, drained yogurt, salt, chilli powder, raisins, cashew nuts and half the fresh coriander and mix well. Shape the mixture into small balls.

3. Heat oil in a *kadai*. Fry one ball; if it comes apart, add some more *besan* to the mixture. Deep-fry the *koftas* till golden brown and drain on absorbent paper.

4. Grind all the ingredients for the *masala* to a fine paste.

5. For the gravy, heat four tablespoons of oil in a pan. Add one cup of ground *masala* and sauté over high heat till aromatic.

6. Add yogurt and one cup of water, salt and sugar and stir till the mixture comes to a boil. Add the remaining fresh leaves coriander.

7. Place the *koftas* in a serving dish, pour the hot gravy over and serve immediately.

Amrud Ki Sabzi

Desi Sabziyan

Ingredients

5-6 medium ripe guavas, peeled and cut into 1-inch pieces
1 tablespoon ghee
A pinch of asafoetida (*hing*)
1 teaspoon *paanch phoron**
¾ teaspoon red chilli powder
Salt to taste
1 tablespoon sugar

* *Paanch phoron is a mixture of equal quantities of mustard seeds, cumin seeds, fenugreek seeds (methi dana), fennel seeds (saunf) and onion seeds (kalonji).*

1. Heat **ghee** in a *kadai*; add asafoetida and *paanch phoron* and sauté till aromatic.

2. Stir in the guavas, red chilli powder, salt and sugar and mix well.

3. Add half a cup of water, cover and cook over low heat for seven to eight minutes or till the guava softens. Serve hot.

CHEF'S TIP
You can cook apples in the same way.

Aloo Posto

Desi Sabziyan

Ingredients

5-6 medium potatoes, peeled and cut into 1-inch pieces
4 tablespoons poppy seeds (*khuskhus*)
2 tablespoons mustard oil
½ teaspoon onion seeds (*kalonji*)
Salt to taste
½ teaspoon sugar
2 green chillies, slit
1 teaspoon ghee (optional)

1 Soak poppy seeds in one cup of warm water for fifteen to twenty minutes. Drain and grind to a smooth paste.

2 Heat mustard oil in a pan to smoking point. Remove from heat, cool and heat the oil again over medium heat. Add *kalonji* and sauté for a few seconds. Add potatoes and cook over medium heat for five minutes, stirring frequently.

3 Stir in the poppy seed paste and half a cup of water; cover and cook over low heat till the potatoes are almost done. Uncover the pan and add salt, sugar and slit green chillies.

4 Continue to cook for one minute more, or till the potatoes are completely cooked. Stir in the ghee and serve hot.

Aluchi Patal Bhaji

Desi Sabziyan

Ingredients

- 8 colocasia leaves (*arbi ke patte*), shredded
- ¼ cup split Bengal gram (*chana dal*), soaked
- Salt to taste
- 3 tablespoons tamarind pulp
- 3 tablespoons oil
- ½ teaspoon mustard seeds
- 5-6 curry leaves
- A generous pinch of asafoetida (*hing*)
- ¼ teaspoon fenugreek seeds (*methi dana*)
- 4 garlic cloves, finely chopped
- 4-5 green chillies, finely chopped
- ¼ teaspoon turmeric powder
- 3 tablespoons gram flour (*besan*)
- ¼ cup raw peanuts (*moongphali*)
- 1 tablespoon grated jaggery
- ½ cup grated fresh coconut

1 Boil *arbi* leaves in four cups of water with *chana dal,* salt and one-and-a-half tablespoons of tamarind pulp till soft.

2 Heat oil in a pan; add mustard seeds, curry leaves, asafoetida, fenugreek seeds and garlic and sauté for one minute. Add green chillies and turmeric powder and

Desi Sabziyan

sauté for half a minute. Stir in the *besan* and sauté for one minute.

3 Add the cooked *arbi* leaves and half a cup of water if necessary. Taste for salt and stir.

4 Add peanuts and more water if necessary. Cook for five minutes and add grated jaggery. Bring to a boil again and stir in the remaining tamarind pulp.

5 Add grated coconut and some more water, if necessary. Cook over medium heat for half an hour, stirring occasionally. Serve hot.

Bataani Kaal Curry

Desi Sabziyan

Ingredients

- ¾ cup shelled green peas, blanched
- 16-20 fresh button mushrooms, blanched and quartered
- ½ cup grated fresh coconut
- ⅕ cup cashew nuts
- 1½ tablespoons oil
- ¾ teaspoon cumin seeds
- ¾ teaspoon mustard seeds
- 1½ tablespoons skinless split black gram (*dhuli urad dal*)
- 2 medium onions, chopped
- ¾ teaspoon ginger paste
- ¾ teaspoon garlic paste
- 1¼ teaspoons coriander powder
- ¾ teaspoon red chilli powder
- ½ teaspoon turmeric powder
- Salt to taste
- 2 medium tomatoes, chopped
- 5-6 curry leaves
- 2 tablespoons fresh coriander leaves, chopped

Desi Sabziyan

1. Grind coconut and cashew nuts with one-fourth cup of water to a fine paste. Wash *urad dal* under running water.

2. Heat oil in a *kadai*. Add cumin seeds, mustard seeds and *urad dal*, and sauté over medium heat until mustard seeds begin to splutter.

3. Add onions and sauté till light brown. Add ginger and garlic pastes and cook for another two minutes.

4. Add coriander powder, chilli powder, turmeric powder, salt and tomatoes and cook till the oil separates.

5. Lower heat, add coconut-cashew nut paste and curry leaves and sauté for one minute. Add two cups of water and bring to a boil, stirring continuously.

6. Add mushrooms and simmer for two minutes.

7. Stir in the green peas and serve hot, garnished with fresh coriander leaves.

Bharwan Karele

Desi Sabziyan

Ingredients

4 medium bitter gourds (*karela*), halved
Salt to taste
1 tablespoon oil
1 medium onion, chopped
2 teaspoons ginger paste
1 tablespoon garlic paste
1 teaspoon coriander powder
½ teaspoon red chilli powder
1 teaspoon cumin powder
½ teaspoon turmeric powder
2 teaspoons tamarind pulp

Stuffing
½ cup gram flour (*besan*)
1 medium onion, chopped
2 tablespoons fresh coriander, chopped
Salt to taste
½ teaspoon red chilli powder
¼ teaspoon *garam masala* powder
1 teaspoon carom seeds (*ajwain*)

1 Scrape the bitter gourds, slit open one side and remove the seeds. Rub salt all over and inside the bitter gourds and set aside for one hour. Wash under running water.

Desi Sabziyan

2 To make the stuffing, dry-roast gram flour in a non-stick pan over low heat till aromatic. Remove from heat, transfer to a plate and leave to cool.

3 Add onion, fresh coriander leaves, salt, chilli powder, *garam masala* powder and carom seeds and mix well. Stuff the *masala* into each bitter gourd and set aside.

4 Heat oil in a pan; add onion and sauté till light golden brown. Add ginger and garlic pastes and sauté for two minutes. Add coriander powder, chilli powder, cumin powder and turmeric powder and sauté till aromatic.

5 Add the stuffed bitter gourds, half a cup of water and salt. Cover and cook over high heat for three to four minutes. Lower heat and cook for ten to twelve minutes, stirring gently from time to time.

6 Stir in the tamarind pulp. Cover once again and simmer for another ten to fifteen minutes, till the bitter gourds are cooked. Serve hot.

Capsicum Kayras

Desi Sabziyan

Ingredients

- 5-6 medium green capsicums, cut into 1-inch cubes
- 2 medium potatoes, peeled and cut into 1-inch cubes
- 1½ tablespoons oil
- ½ teaspoon mustard seeds
- A pinch of asafoetida (*hing*)
- ½ cup peanuts (*moongphali*)
- ¼ teaspoon turmeric powder
- Salt to taste
- 1½ tablespoons grated jaggery

Masala
- ½ cup grated fresh coconut
- 3 tablespoons sesame seeds (*til*)
- ½ tablespoon oil
- 2 tablespoons split Bengal gram (*chana dal*)
- 2 tablespoons coriander seeds
- ¼ teaspoon fenugreek seeds (*methi dana*)
- 4-5 dried red chillies (*sookhi lal mirch*), preferably Bedgi
- 2 tablespoons tamarind pulp

1 For the *masala*, dry-roast the grated coconut and sesame seeds separately and set aside. Heat half a tablespoon of oil in a pan; add *chana dal*, coriander seeds, fenugreek seeds and red chillies and sauté till aromatic. Grind spices with roasted coconut, sesame seeds, tamarind pulp and three-fourth cup of water to a fine paste.

Desi Sabziyan

2 Heat oil in a separate pan and add mustard seeds. When the mustard seeds begin to splutter, add asafoetida, stir and add peanuts; sauté for three to four minutes.

3 Add the potatoes, turmeric powder, salt and jaggery. Stir, cover and cook over low heat for five minutes. Add capsicums, stir and cook till the vegetables are half-done.

4 Add the ground paste, one-and-a-half cups of water and simmer for three to four minutes. Serve hot.

CHEF'S TIP

If Bedgi chillies are not available, use Kashmiri chillies to prepare this Saraswat Brahmin wedding delicacy.

Batata Nu Shaak

Desi Sabziyan

Ingredients

- 5 large potatoes
- 1 tablespoon oil + for deep-frying
- 1 tablespoon sesame seeds (*til*), roasted
- 1 teaspoon red chilli powder
- ¼ teaspoon turmeric powder
- 1½ teaspoons coriander powder
- 1 tablespoon lemon juice
- ½ teaspoon sugar
- Salt to taste
- 2 tablespoons fresh coriander leaves, chopped

1. Peel and cut potatoes into half-inch thick round slices. Cut each slice into thin strips and soak in water. Drain thoroughly.

2. Heat oil in a *kadai* and deep-fry potatoes till golden brown. Drain on absorbent paper.

3. Heat one tablespoon of oil in a pan and add sesame seeds. When they begin to change colour, add fried potatoes, red chilli powder, turmeric powder, coriander powder, lemon juice, sugar and salt. Mix well and cook for two minutes.

4. Garnish with fresh coriander leaves and serve hot.

Pyaaz Ki Tarkari

Desi Sabziyan

Ingredients

8 medium onions, chopped
8 spring onions, quartered
3 tablespoons oil
1 teaspoon ginger paste
1 teaspoon garlic paste

Salt to taste
½ teaspoon turmeric powder
1 teaspoon red chilli powder
2 tablespoons tamarind pulp
5 spring onion greens stalks, chopped

1 Heat oil in a *kadai*; add chopped onions and cook till golden.

2 Add ginger paste and garlic paste and sauté for one minute.

3 Add salt, turmeric powder, chilli powder, spring onions and one-third cup of water. When the mixture begins to boil, lower heat and simmer for two to three minutes.

4 Stir in the tamarind pulp and cook for one minute.

5 Serve hot, garnished with spring onion greens.

Chorchori

Desi Sabziyan

Ingredients

- ¼ medium cauliflower, separated into florets
- 2 medium potatoes, peeled and cut into ½-inch pieces
- 1 medium sweet potato, peeled and cut into ½-inch pieces
- 100 grams red pumpkin (*kaddu*), peeled and cut into ½-inch pieces
- 1 medium brinjal, cut into ½-inch pieces
- 6-8 French beans, cut into ½-inch pieces
- 6-8 spinach leaves, shredded
- 1½ tablespoon mustard oil
- 1½ teaspoons *paanch phoron* (page 15)
- ½ teaspoon red chilli powder
- ¼ teaspoon turmeric powder
- 2 green chillies, slit
- ½ teaspoon sugar
- Salt to taste

1 Heat one tablespoon of mustard oil in a pan till smoking point. Remove from heat, cool and heat once again over medium heat.

2 Add *paanch phoron* and when the spices begin to splutter, stir in the chilli powder.

Desi Sabziyan

3 Add the vegetables, turmeric powder, slit green chillies, sugar and salt to taste. Lower heat, cover and cook, stirring occasionally, for eight to ten minutes, or till the potatoes are cooked.

4 Add the remaining mustard oil and sauté for one minute till the *chorchori* is dry.

CHEF'S TIP

Mustard oil is heated to smoking point and cooled before using it for cooking, to minimise its strong smell and taste.

Khoya Matar

Desi Sabziyan

Ingredients

½ cup *khoya/mawa*, crumbled
1½ cups shelled green peas
3 tablespoons oil
1 teaspoon cumin seeds
2 medium onions, chopped
½ teaspoon red chilli powder
2 teaspoons coriander powder
½ teaspoon fennel (*saunf*) powder
1 teaspoon *garam masala* powder
Salt to taste
2 green chillies, chopped
2 medium tomatoes, chopped
8 cashew nuts, chopped
2 tablespoons fresh coriander leaves, chopped

1. Heat oil in a heavy-bottomed pan; add cumin seeds, and when they begin to change colour, add onions and sauté till golden. Add *khoya* and stir continuously till the *khoya* changes colour. Lower heat to medium.

2. Add red chilli powder, coriander powder, fennel powder and *garam masala* powder and salt. Mix well.

3. Add green peas, green chillies, tomatoes and half a cup of water and cook till the oil separates.

4. Serve hot, garnished with cashew nuts and fresh coriander leaves.

Mirchi Ka Salan

Desi Sabziyan

Ingredients

- 18-20 large green chillies
- 2 tablespoons oil + for deep-frying
- 2 tablespoons sesame seeds (*til*)
- 1 tablespoon coriander seeds
- 1 teaspoon cumin seeds
- ½ cup roasted peanuts
- 2 dried red chillies
- 1 inch ginger, roughly chopped
- 6-8 garlic cloves, roughly chopped
- 1 teaspoon mustard seeds
- 8-10 curry leaves
- 1 medium onion, grated
- 1 teaspoon turmeric powder
- 2 tablespoons tamarind pulp
- Salt to taste

1 Wash, wipe and slit green chillies lengthways without cutting them into two. Deep-fry in hot oil for one minute. Drain on absorbent paper and set aside.

2 Dry-roast sesame seeds, coriander seeds and cumin seeds separately. Grind together the roasted seeds, peanuts, red chillies, ginger and garlic to a paste.

3 Heat two tablespoons of oil in a pan; add mustard seeds. When they begin to splutter, add curry leaves and grated onion and sauté till light golden brown.

Desi Sabziyan

4 Add turmeric powder and mix well. Add *masala* paste and cook for three minutes, stirring continuously. Stir in one-and-a-half cups of water and bring to a boil. Lower heat and simmer for ten minutes.

5 Add tamarind pulp, dissolved in half a cup of water if it is too thick.

6 Add fried green chillies and salt and cook over low heat for eight to ten minutes.

CHEF'S TIP

In Hyderabad, *Mirchi ka Salan* is traditionally served as an accompaniment to *biryanis*. Some people like to add grated coconut to the *masala* paste, but I prefer it without. This gravy is referred to as "*tili aur falli*" gravy (*til*=sesame seeds, *moongphali*= peanuts).

Batata Song

Desi Sabziyan

Ingredients

4 large potatoes, boiled, peeled and cubed
8-10 dried red chillies, seeded
1 lemon-sized ball tamarind
3 tablespoons coconut oil

2 large onions, chopped
Salt to taste

1. Lightly roast red chillies; grind with tamarind and a little water to a fine paste.

2. Heat oil in a frying-pan and fry the onions until light brown.

3. Add the ground paste and sauté for two to three minutes.

4. Add the potatoes and mix well. Add one cup of water and salt and simmer over low heat till the gravy thickens.

5. Serve hot with *puris* or *chapatis*

CHEF'S TIP

If you do not like the flavour of coconut oil, use any refined oil.

Gobhi Mussallam

Desi Sabziyan

Ingredients

- 2 small cauliflowers
- ½ cup + 1 teaspoon melon seeds (*magaz*)
- Salt to taste
- 1½ teaspoon turmeric powder
- 2 tablespoons oil
- 2 medium onions, grated
- 1 tablespoon ginger paste
- 1 tablespoon garlic paste
- 1 teaspoon cumin powder
- 1 tablespoon red chilli powder
- 1 tablespoon coriander powder
- 1 teaspoon *garam masala* powder
- ½ cup tomato purée
- ½ cup *khoya/mawa*
- ½ cup fresh cream
- 2 tablespoons chopped fresh coriander leaves

1 Soak half a cup of melon seeds in water for one hour; grind seeds to a smooth paste.

2 Remove the cauliflower stalks. Boil whole cauliflowers in salted water with half a teaspoon of turmeric powder till half-cooked.

3 Heat oil in a *kadai*; add grated onions and sauté till golden brown.

4 Add ginger paste, garlic paste, cumin powder, chilli powder, coriander powder, remaining turmeric powder, *garam masala* powder and salt. Sauté for half a minute.

5 Add tomato purée and cook till the oil separates. Add melon seed paste dissolved in one cup of water; bring to a boil and stir in the *khoya*.

6 Add parboiled cauliflower and cook, covered, over low heat for fifteen minutes.

7 Stir in the fresh cream and simmer for five minutes.

8 Serve hot, garnished with chopped coriander leaves and remaining melon seeds.

Guar Ki Sabzi

Desi Sabziyan

Ingredients

- 1½ cups (100 grams) dried cluster beans (*guar*)
- 3 tablespoons mustard oil
- 1 bay leaf
- ½ teaspoon cumin seeds
- 5-6 dried red chillies, broken into bits
- A pinch of asafoetida (*hing*)
- ½ teaspoon mustard powder
- Salt to taste
- 3 tablespoons yogurt, whisked
- 1 teaspoon red chilli powder
- ½ teaspoon turmeric powder
- 1 tablespoon *garam masala* powder
- ½ teaspoon dried mango powder (*amchur*)
- 1 teaspoon coriander powder
- ½ teaspoon sugar
- 2-3 pieces dried mango, soaked

1 Soak cluster beans in four cups of water for one hour. Drain.

2 Heat mustard oil in a pan. Stir in the bay leaf, cumin seeds, red chillies, asafoetida and mustard powder.

3 Add the drained beans and salt. Mix well and sir in the yogurt.

4 Mix all the powdered spices and sugar with a little water and add to the vegetable. Add the dried mango pieces and cook till dry. Serve hot.

Bhindi Coconut Masala

Desi Sabziyan

Ingredients

- 500 grams ladies' fingers (*bhindi*) cut into ¾-inch pieces
- 2 teaspoons oil
- 7-8 garlic cloves, crushed
- 2-3 dried red chillies (*sookhi lal mirch*) preferably Bedgi)
- 1 teaspoon mustard seeds
- ½ teaspoon fenugreek seeds (*methi dana*)
- 1 teaspoon coriander seeds
- ½ cup grated fresh coconut
- 1 tablespoon tamarind pulp
- Salt to taste

1. Heat two tablespoons of oil in a *kadai*. Add crushed garlic and sauté till golden. Add ladies' fingers, stir well and cook, uncovered, for three to four minutes.

2. Heat two teaspoons of oil in a small pan. Add the whole red chillies, mustard seeds, fenugreek seeds and coriander seeds; sauté till lightly coloured. Grind these spices with grated coconut to a slightly coarse paste. Add tamarind pulp and grind again.

3. Add the ground *masala* to the ladies' fingers, stir well and cook for two minutes.

4. Stir in two cups of water and salt to taste and cook till the gravy thickens. Serve hot.

Tameta Ganthia Nu Shaak

Desi Sabziyan

Ingredients

Ganthia
½ cup gram flour (*besan*)
Salt to taste
¼ teaspoon turmeric powder
½ teaspoon red chilli powder
¼ teaspoon carom seeds (*ajwain*)

Gravy
5 medium tomatoes, chopped
2 tablespoons oil
A pinch of asafoetida (*hing*)
½ teaspoon mustard seeds
½ teaspoon cumin seeds
Salt to taste
1½ teaspoons coriander powder
1 teaspoon cumin powder
½ teaspoon turmeric powder
1 teaspoon red chilli powder
1 tablespoon grated jaggery

Desi Sabziyan

1. To make *ganthia*, mix together gram flour, salt, turmeric powder, chilli powder and carom seeds with enough water to make a hard dough. Add a little oil, if desired, and knead again.

2. Roll the dough into thin cylinders and cut them into half-inch long pieces. Roll the pieces between your palms till smooth. Set aside.

3. To make the gravy, heat oil in a pan. Add asafoetida, mustard seeds and cumin seeds. When the seeds begin to change colour add tomatoes, salt and one-and-a-half cups of water.

4. Add coriander powder, cumin powder, turmeric powder and chilli powder. When the gravy begins to boil, gently slide in the *ganthia*.

5. Add jaggery and stir gently. Cook for ten to twelve minutes over medium heat.

6. Serve hot.

Kachchi Makai Dhingri

Desi Sabziyan

Ingredients

- 10-12 babycorn cobs, cut into ½-inch pieces
- 10-12 medium fresh button mushrooms, quartered
- ½ cup sweetcorn kernels
- 1 inch ginger, chopped
- 6-8 garlic cloves, chopped
- 4 tablespoons oil
- 2 bay leaves
- 1 medium onion, grated
- 2 green chillies, slit and seeded
- 1 tablespoon red chilli powder
- 3 tablespoons coriander powder
- 1 teaspoon turmeric powder
- ½ teaspoon cumin powder
- 1 medium tomato, finely chopped
- 1 medium green capsicum, cut into ½-inch wide strips
- Salt to taste
- 1 teaspoon *garam masala* powder
- ½ cup fresh coriander leaves, chopped

Desi Sabziyan

1. Grind ginger and garlic to a fine paste.

2. Heat oil in a pan; add bay leaves, grated onion and slit green chillies. Sauté for three to four minutes or until the onion turns light brown. Add ginger-garlic paste and sauté for a few seconds.

3. Add chilli powder, coriander powder, turmeric powder and cumin powder. Mix well and add chopped tomato. Cook over high heat for two to three minutes, stirring continuously. Add mushrooms, babycorn, sweetcorn and salt to taste, and continue to cook for five minutes over medium heat.

4. Add capsicum, toss well and cook for two minutes over medium heat, stirring continuously.

5. Sprinkle chopped coriander leaves and *garam masala* powder and serve hot.

Ker Sangri

Desi Sabziyan

Ingredients

½ cup desert berries (*ker*)
1 cup dried desert beans (*sangri*)
1 cup + 4 teaspoons yogurt
4 tablespoons oil
1 teaspoon cumin seeds
5-6 dried red chillies, broken into pieces
1 teaspoon garlic paste
1 teaspoon ginger paste
½ teaspoon turmeric powder
1 teaspoon red chilli powder
1 teaspoon coriander powder
5-6 dried mango pieces
Salt to taste
1 teaspoon mango powder (*amchur*)
1 tablespoon fresh coriander leaves, chopped
1 tablespoon chopped and fried garlic

1 Soak the berries and the dried beans in one cup of beaten yogurt overnight. Drain and rinse under running water.

2 Boil together the berries and beans in salted water for fifteen to twenty minutes. Drain.

Desi Sabziyan

3 Heat oil in a *kadai*; add cumin seeds, red chillies, garlic and ginger pastes and sauté for a few seconds. Add a little water, turmeric powder, chilli powder and coriander powder and mix well. Add dried mango and four teaspoons of yogurt and stir to mix.

4 Stir in the *ker*, *sangri*, salt, *amchur* and fresh coriander leaves.

5 Serve with fried garlic.

CHEF'S TIP

Once famine food, these fruits of the dessert have achieved cult status as Rajasthani delicacies. Soaking them in yogurt, before cooking adds flavour and moistness.

Methi Papad Ki Sabzi

Desi Sabziyan

Ingredients

- 8 *moong dal papads*
- ¼ cup fenugreek seeds (*methi dana*)
- Salt to taste
- 2 tablespoons oil
- 1 teaspoon mustard seeds
- 2 inches cinnamon
- 4-5 dried red chillies, broken into bits
- A pinch of asafoetida (*hing*)
- ½ teaspoon turmeric powder
- 2 teaspoons coriander powder
- 1½ teaspoons red chilli powder
- 3-4 pieces of *kokum*
- 1½ tablespoons grated jaggery
- 2 tablespoons fresh coriander leaves, chopped

1 Soak fenugreek seeds in two cups of water for two hours. Drain and pressure-cook with two cups of water and salt till almost done. Wash under running water to remove the bitterness. Drain.

2 Heat oil in a *kadai*; add mustard seeds, cinnamon and red chillies and sauté for half a minute. Add asafoetida, turmeric powder, coriander powder, chilli powder and cooked fenugreek seeds. Sauté for a few seconds.

3 Add two cups of water and bring to a boil.

4 Add salt, *kokum* and jaggery to the pan, and simmer for three to four minutes.

5 Cut *papads* into finger-sized strips and add to the *kadai*. Stir, cover and cook over low heat till the *papads* soften.

6 Add chopped coriander leaves, stir and serve hot.

CHEF'S TIP

Fenugreek seeds are actually legumes and therefore high in protein. They are also rich in vitamins and minerals.

Tender Coconut And Cashew Nut Sukke — *Desi Sabziyan*

Ingredients

- 1 cup tender coconut flesh, cut into 2-inch by ¼-inch slices
- 25-30 cashew nuts, soaked for 1 hour
- 1 tablespoon oil
- ½ teaspoon cumin seeds
- 3-4 garlic cloves, crushed
- 1 large onion, chopped
- 5-6 curry leaves
- 2 medium tomatoes, chopped
- ½ teaspoon turmeric powder
- 1 teaspoon red chilli powder
- Sea salt to taste
- 3 tablespoons tomato purée
- 2 tablespoons grated fresh coconut
- ½ cup thick coconut milk (page 94)
- A few sprigs of fresh coriander leaves, chopped

1 Heat oil in a pan; add cumin seeds, crushed garlic and chopped onion and sauté till onion is lightly browned.

2 Add curry leaves, chopped tomatoes, turmeric powder and chilli powder and cook for a few minutes.

Desi Sabziyan

3 Add the soaked cashew nuts and a little water. Cook for a few minutes, and stir in the sea salt and tomato purée.

4 Mix in the tender coconut and grated coconut. Stir in the coconut milk and cook till almost dry.

5 Add chopped coriander leaves and mix well. Serve hot.

CHEF'S TIP

Choose green unripe coconuts. Shave off the top with a sharp knife, making a small hole to drain out the coconut water. Widen the opening and scoop out the soft flesh. Chill the coconut water for a deliciously refreshing nutritious drink.

Mixed Vegetables In Coconut Milk

Desi Sabziyan

Ingredients

- 2 medium potatoes, peeled and cut into 1-inch cubes
- 12-15 broad beans (*sem ki phalli/papdi*), cut into 1-inch pieces
- ½ cup shelled green peas
- ¼ medium cauliflower, separated into florets
- 2 medium carrots, cut into 1-inch cubes
- 100 grams red pumpkin (*kaddu*), peeled and cut into 1-inch cubes
- 1½ cups grated fresh coconut
- 2 tablespoons tamarind pulp
- 3 tablespoons groundnut oil
- 4 dried red chillies
- 1 teaspoon cumin seeds
- 1 tablespoon coriander seeds
- 8-10 garlic cloves, peeled
- 1 teaspoon turmeric powder
- Salt to taste
- 1 teaspoon mustard seeds
- 1 teaspoon split black gram (*urad dal*)
- 8-10 curry leaves

1 Add warm water to one cup of grated coconut and squeeze to extract thick and thin milk. Mix the tamarind pulp in half a cup of water.

2 Heat a little oil in a pan; sauté two dried red chillies, cumin seeds, coriander seeds, garlic and the remaining grated coconut till aromatic. Grind with a little water to a fine paste. Set aside.

Desi Sabziyan

3 Boil the vegetables in the thin coconut milk with turmeric powder, tamarind paste and salt till three-fourth cooked. Add the ground *masala* and cook for ten minutes.

4 Heat the remaining oil in a separate pan; add the remaining red chillies, broken into two, mustard seeds and *urad dal*. Stir in the curry leaves and pour the sizzling spices over the vegetables.

5 Cook till the vegetables are done. Add the thick coconut milk and simmer for two to three minutes. Serve hot with boiled rice.

CHEF'S TIP

If broad beans are not available, replace them with French beans.

Nadir Yakhni

Desi Sabziyan

Ingredients

- 500 grams lotus stems (*nadir/kamal kakri/bhen*)
- Salt to taste
- Oil for deep-frying
- 2 medium onions, sliced
- 2 cups yogurt
- 2 tablespoons ghee
- 2 black cardamoms
- 4-6 cloves
- 2 one-inch sticks cinnamon
- 1 teaspoon fennel (*saunf*) powder
- 1 teaspoon dried ginger powder (*sonth*)
- 4-6 green cardamoms
- ½ teaspoon caraway seeds (*shahi jeera*)
- A big pinch of dried mint leaves, crushed

1 Peel and wash lotus stems thoroughly under running water and cut diagonally into three-fourth-inch pieces.

2 Bring four cups of water to a boil in a pan; add lotus stems and salt and cook till half-done.

3 Heat oil in a *kadai* and deep-fry onions till brown. Cool and grind onions, with a little water if necessary, to a smooth paste.

4 Mix yogurt with half a cup of water. Strain through a piece of muslin.

Desi Sabziyan

5 Cook the strained yogurt mixture over high heat, stirring continuously, till the mixture changes colour. Remove from heat.

6 Heat ghee in a pan; add black cardamoms, cloves and cinnamon and sauté till the spices sizzle.

7 Mix fennel powder and dried ginger powder with one cup of water. Add the brown onion paste and mix well.

8 Stir the mixture into the pan. Add cooked yogurt and lotus stems and mix well.

9 Add salt and green cardamoms. Cook till lotus stems are completely cooked.

10 Stir in the caraway seeds and dried mint leaves, remove from heat and serve hot.

Sai Bhaji

Desi Sabziyan

Ingredients

- 2 medium bunches (400 grams) spinach
- ½ medium bunch *khatta* leaves
- 4 tablespoons oil
- ½ teaspoon cumin seeds
- 2 medium onions, finely chopped
- 1 inch ginger, peeled and finely chopped
- 3-4 green chillies, finely chopped
- 2 small-sized long brinjals, cut into 1-inch cubes
- 2 medium potatoes, peeled and cut into 1-inch cubes
- 4 tablespoons split Bengal gram (*chana dal*), soaked
- 2 large tomatoes, roughly chopped
- ¼ teaspoon turmeric powder
- 1 teaspoon red chilli powder
- Salt to taste

1 Cut the spinach and half the *khatta* leaves into fine shreds.

2 Heat oil in a pressure cooker and add cumin seeds. When they begin to change

Desi Sabziyan

colour add onions and sauté till golden brown.

3 Add ginger and green chillies and sauté for a few seconds. Add a little water if required.

4 Add spinach, whole *khatta* leaves, shredded *khatta* leaves, brinjal and potato cubes, soaked *chana dal*, tomatoes, turmeric powder, chilli powder and salt.

5 Stir in two cups of water. Pressure-cook over high heat till pressure is released once (one whistle). Lower heat and cook for eight to ten minutes more.

6 Remove the potato cubes with a slotted spoon and pureé the remaining mixture with a hand blender. Add the potato cubes and serve hot.

Palak Chaman

Desi Sabziyan

Ingredients

- 2 cups spinach purée
- 150 grams cottage cheese (*paneer*), cut into 1-inch cubes
- 2 medium carrots, cut into ½-inch cubes
- 10 French beans, cut into ½-inch pieces
- ½ medium cauliflower, separated into small florets
- ½ cup shelled green peas
- ½ bunch fenugreek leaves (*methi*), chopped
- 1 tablespoon oil
- ½ teaspoon cumin seeds
- 2 medium onions, chopped
- 1 teaspoon ginger paste
- 1 teaspoon garlic paste
- ¼ teaspoon turmeric powder
- 2 medium tomatoes, chopped
- ½ teaspoon red chilli powder
- 1 teaspoon coriander powder
- Salt to taste
- ½ teaspoon *garam masala* powder
- 2 tablespoons cream (*malai*)

Desi Sabziyan

1. Parboil carrots, French beans, cauliflower and green peas separately.

2. Heat oil in pan; add cumin seeds; when they begin to change colour, add onions and sauté till golden. Add ginger paste and garlic paste and continue to sauté for a few seconds

3. Stir in the turmeric powder and tomatoes and sauté for a few minutes. Add chilli powder and coriander powder, and sauté till the oil begins to separate.

4. Add fenugreek leaves and sauté for a minute or two.

5. Stir in the parboiled vegetables; add the spinach purée and salt. Cook for one minute. Add *paneer* and *garam masala* powder and simmer for two to three minutes.

6. Serve, garnished with swirls of cream.

Sweet And Sour Tomatoes

Desi Sabziyan

Ingredients

- 250 grams ripe tomatoes, cut into ½-inch pieces
- 2 teaspoons oil
- ¼ teaspoon mustard seeds
- 2-3 green chillies, slit
- A pinch of asafoetida (*hing*)
- ¼ teaspoon turmeric powder
- Salt to taste
- 2 teaspoons grated jaggery
- ¼ cup peanuts, roasted and crushed
- A few sprigs of fresh coriander leaves, chopped

1 Heat oil in a *kadai* and add mustard seeds. When they begin to splutter, add green chillies. Sauté for half a minute and add asafoetida and turmeric powder.

2 Add tomatoes, salt and jaggery and stir well to mix. Cover, lower heat and cook till the tomatoes soften.

3 Add crushed peanuts and mix well.

4 Garnish with chopped coriander leaves and serve hot.

Urulai Chettinadu

Desi Sabziyan

Ingredients

500 grams baby potatoes, halved
4 dried red chillies
2 tablespoons skinless split black gram (*dhuli urad dal*)
10-12 black peppercorns
5 tablespoons oil
1 teaspoon mustard seeds
20 curry leaves
20 small onions, peeled
Salt to taste

1. Dry-roast red chillies, *urad dal* and peppercorns. Cool and pound to a coarse powder.

2. Heat oil in a *kadai*; add mustard seeds, curry leaves and small onions, and sauté till lightly browned.

3. Stir in the potatoes and add salt. Cover and cook till the potatoes are almost done.

4. Add the *masala* powder and mix well. Cover and cook over low heat for about three to four minutes or till the potatoes are cooked. Serve hot.

Dhaabe Ki Sabziyan

Desi Sabziyan

Ingredients

- 10-12 cauliflower florets
- 2 medium potatoes, boiled, peeled and cut into 1-inch cubes
- ½ cup shelled green peas
- ½ teaspoon turmeric powder
- 4 tablespoons oil + for deep-frying
- ½ teaspoon cumin seeds
- 10-12 garlic cloves, minced
- 2 medium onions, grated
- 2 medium tomatoes, grated
- 1½ teaspoons grated ginger
- 2 teaspoons coriander powder
- ½ teaspoon roasted cumin powder
- 1½ teaspoon red chilli powder
- 2 tablespoons fresh coriander leaves, chopped
- Salt to taste
- 1 teaspoon *garam masala* powder

Dal-fry

- 1 cup split pigeon peas (*arhar/toovar dal*), boiled
- 1 tablespoon butter
- ½ teaspoon cumin seeds
- ½ teaspoon red chilli powder

Desi Sabziyan

1. Boil the cauliflower in one cup of water with a quarter teaspoon of turmeric powder for two to three minutes. Drain.

2. Boil green peas in one cup of water. Drain and refresh in cold water. Drain.

3. Wash and soak the *arhar dal* in two cups of water for half an hour. Drain and boil with three cups of water till soft.

4. Heat sufficient oil in a *kadai* and deep-fry the boiled cauliflower florets and potato cubes. Drain on absorbent paper.

5. Heat four tablespoons of oil in a *kadai* and add cumin seeds. When they change colour, add half the garlic and sauté till reddish brown. Add onions and continue to sauté till brown.

6. Add tomatoes, ginger, remaining turmeric powder, coriander powder, roasted cumin powder and red chilli powder. Sauté till the oil separates. Remove from heat and set aside.

7. For the *dal-fry*, heat butter in a separate pan; stir in the cumin seeds, chilli powder, remaining garlic and half the

prepared gravy. Add the boiled *dal* and salt to taste. Bring to a boil, lower heat and simmer for two to three minutes. Stir in half the coriander leaves

8 Add boiled peas, fried potatoes and cauliflower to the remaining gravy. Mix well and cook over low heat for two to three minutes. Stir in the remaining coriander leaves.

9 Sprinkle *garam masala* powder and serve.

Vegetable Ishtew

Desi Sabziyan

Ingredients

- 2 medium carrots, cubed
- 2 medium potatoes, peeled and cubed
- 7-8 cauliflower florets
- 6–8 French beans, cut into 1-inch pieces
- 2 tablespoons coconut oil
- 2 bay leaves
- 2 one-inch sticks cinnamon
- 4 cloves
- 2 star anise (*chakri phool/badiyan*)
- 10-12 curry leaves
- 4 green chillies, slit
- 2 medium onions, chopped
- 2 teaspoons ginger-garlic paste
- 1 cup thin coconut milk (see below)
- Salt to taste
- 1 cup thick coconut milk (see below)
- A pinch of *garam masala* powder

1 Parboil carrots, potatoes, cauliflower and French beans separately. Drain and set aside.

2 Heat coconut oil in a deep pan. Add the bay leaves, cinnamon, cloves, star anise, curry leaves, green chillies and onions. Sauté for two minutes.

Desi Sabziyan

3 Stir in the ginger-garlic paste and cook for one minute.

4 Add carrots, potatoes and cauliflower and thin coconut milk. Cook for two to three minutes and add salt and French beans. Cook till French beans are tender.

5 Stir in the thick coconut milk and a pinch of *garam masala* powder. Immediately turn off the heat. Serve hot with *appams*.

CHEF'S TIP

To extract 1 cup of thick coconut milk, process 1 cup of fresh grated coconut with half a cup of warm water in a blender. Press through a fine strainer or piece of muslin. For thin coconut milk, process the coconut once more with 1 cup of warm water. Strain.

Shahi Dhingri Matar Paneer

Desi Sabziyan

Ingredients

- 10-15 fresh button mushrooms, halved
- 1 cup shelled green peas, boiled
- 100 grams cottage cheese (*paneer*), cut into ½-inch cubes
- Oil for deep-frying
- 2 large onions, sliced
- 10 cashew nuts
- 2 tablespoons ghee
- 3 green cardamoms
- 1 black cardamom
- 3 cloves
- 1 inch cinnamon
- 6-8 black peppercorns
- 1 bay leaf
- 1½ tablespoons *khoya/mawa*, grated
- ¼ teaspoon turmeric powder
- 1 teaspoon red chilli powder
- ½ cup yogurt
- 2 teaspoons coriander powder
- ½ teaspoon cumin powder
- Salt to taste
- 3 tablespoons fresh cream
- 1 teaspoon *garam masala* powder

Desi Sabziyan

1. Heat oil in a *kadai* and deep-fry the sliced onions till well browned. Cool slightly and grind to a fine paste. Grind cashew nuts with a little water to a fine paste.

2. Heat ghee in a pan; add green cardamoms, black cardamom, cloves, cinnamon, peppercorns and bay leaf. When the spices begin to sizzle, add mushrooms and sauté for a few minutes.

3. Add *khoya* and sauté for two minutes.

4. Add brown onion paste and cashew nut paste and sauté for a few seconds.

5. Add turmeric powder and chilli powder and mix well. Stir in the yogurt, mix well and cook for two to three minutes.

6. Add coriander powder, cumin powder and salt and mix well. Add boiled peas and cook for three to four minutes.

7. Stir in the fresh cream and *paneer* cubes and sprinkle with *garam masala* powder. Stir gently and serve hot.

Ennai Kathrikai

Desi Sabziyan

Ingredients

16-20 baby brinjals
¼ cup groundnut oil
10 curry leaves
1 tablespoon tamarind pulp

Masala Powder
2 tablespoons groundnut oil
½ teaspoon mustard seeds
½ teaspoon cumin seeds
¼ teaspoon fenugreek seeds (*methi dana*)
2 tablespoons coriander seeds
1 tablespoon split Bengal gram (*chana dal*)
1 tablespoon split black gram (*urad dal*)
4 dried red chillies
10 black peppercorns
¼ teaspoon asafoetida (*hing*)
¼ teaspoon turmeric powder
10-12 curry leaves, finely chopped
½ cup grated fresh coconut
Salt to taste

Desi Sabziyan

1. Trim the head of the brinjals and slit into four without separating the segments.

2. Heat two tablespoons of oil and fry mustard seeds, cumin seeds, fenugreek seeds, coriander seeds, *chana dal* and *urad dal*. Add red chillies, peppercorns, asafoetida, turmeric powder and curry leaves. Remove from heat and mix in the coconut. Grind coarsely when completely cold and add salt.

3. Fill the slit brinjals with the *masala*.

4. Heat a quarter cup of oil in a *kadai*; add curry leaves and stuffed brinjals. Spread any remaining *masala* over the brinjals, cover and cook for a few minutes.

5. Mix the tamarind pulp with a little water and stir into the brinjals. Add another quarter cup of water if the dish is too dry. Cover and cook over medium heat for fifteen or twenty minutes. Serve hot.

Tawa Vegetables

Desi Sabziyan

Ingredients

- 4 small brinjals, slit into four
- 2 bitter gourds (*karela*), halved, cored, and cut into four
- 4 medium *parwars*, slit into four
- 8 *tindli*, slit into four
- 8 baby potatoes, boiled and peeled
- 8 button (pearl) onions
- 8 fresh button mushrooms, quartered
- 8 ladies' fingers (*bhindi*), slit into four
- 4 tablespoons oil + for deep-frying
- 4 medium onions, chopped
- 3 inches ginger, chopped
- 6-8 green chillies, seeded and chopped
- 8 teaspoons *pav bhaji masala*
- Salt to taste
- 16 tablespoons tomato purée
- 4 tablespoons fresh coriander leaves, chopped

1 Heat oil in a *kadai* and deep-fry brinjals and *karela* till lightly browned. Drain.

2 Add *parwar* and *tindli* to the same oil and deep-fry till lightly browned. Drain.

3 Deep-fry baby potatoes, button onions, mushrooms and ladies' fingers one after the other. Drain.

Desi Sabziyan

4 Heat a *tawa*. Arrange the fried vegetables around the edge of the *tawa*.

5 For each portion, heat one tablespoon of oil, add a quarter of the chopped onions and sauté till brown. Add a quarter of the ginger and continue to sauté.

6 Add a little water to the *tawa* and stir. Add a quarter of the green chillies and sauté for a few seconds.

7 Add a quarter of each vegetable to the *masala*. Add two teaspoons of *pav bhaji masala*, salt, four tablespoons of tomato purée and a little water and mix well.

8 Cook for three to four minutes, garnish with coriander leaves and serve hot.

Wadian Aloo

Desi Sabziyan

Ingredients

- 2-3 large dried *urad dal* nuggets (*wadian*)
- 4 medium potatoes
- 2 one-inch pieces ginger
- 5 tablespoons oil
- 1 teaspoon cumin seeds
- 1 large onion, chopped
- A pinch of asafoetida (*hing*)
- ½ teaspoon turmeric powder
- 2 teaspoons coriander powder
- ½ teaspoon cumin powder
- 1½ teaspoons red chilli powder
- Salt to taste
- 2 large tomatoes, finely chopped
- 2 green chillies, slit
- ½ teaspoon *garam masala* powder
- A few sprigs of fresh coriander leaves, chopped

1 Break *wadian* into small pieces.

2 Wash and cut unpeeled potatoes into eight pieces each.

3 Finely chop one piece of ginger and cut the other into fine strips.

4 Heat three tablespoons of oil in a pan; add *wadian* and roast till aromatic.

Desi Sabziyan

Drain on absorbent paper and soak in one cup of water.

5 Heat two tablespoons of oil in a separate pan; add cumin seeds and onion and sauté for three minutes.

6 Add potatoes, chopped ginger, asafoetida, turmeric powder, coriander powder, cumin powder, chilli powder and salt and mix well.

7 Stir in three cups of water. Add *wadian*, cover and cook till potatoes are done.

8 Add tomatoes and slit green chillies and cook for five minutes.

9 Sprinkle with *garam masala* powder, ginger strips and chopped coriander leaves and serve hot.

CHEF'S TIP

If available, use *wadian* from *Amritsar*, which are also delicious but very spicy!

Manje Kael

Desi Sabziyan

Ingredients

- ½ kilogram medium kohlrabi (*knol-khol*), peeled and cut into 1-inch pieces
- 2 teaspoons salt + to taste
- 3 tablespoons oil + for deep-frying
- 1 teaspoon cumin seeds
- 6 green cardamoms
- 3 black cardamoms
- 2 inches cinnamon
- 2 medium onions, peeled and sliced
- 1 teaspoon garlic paste
- ¼ teaspoon turmeric powder
- 1 teaspoon dried ginger powder (*sonth*)
- 2 teaspoons Kashmiri chilli powder
- 1½ cups yogurt, whisked
- 1 tablespoon fresh coriander leaves, chopped

1 Mix the *knol-khol* pieces with two teaspoons of salt and set aside for five minutes. Wash and drain.

2 Heat oil in a *kadai* and deep-fry the *knol-khol* till light brown. Drain on absorbent paper.

3 Heat three tablespoons of oil in a non-stick pan; add cumin seeds and stir-fry for thirty seconds. Add green cardamoms, black cardamoms and cinnamon, and stir-fry for two to three minutes.

Desi Sabziyan

4 Add onions and stir-fry over medium heat till they turn golden brown.

5 Add garlic paste and stir-fry for one or two minutes; stir in the turmeric powder and dried ginger powder.

6 Add chilli powder mixed with half a cup of water, and bring the mixture to a boil. Add fried *knol-khol*, yogurt and salt to taste. Cook till most of the liquid evaporates, making sure the yogurt does not curdle.

7 Serve hot, garnished with coriander leaves.

Sarson Ka Saag

Desi Sabziyan

Ingredients

- 2 medium bunches (450 grams) fresh mustard leaves (*sarson ka saag*)
- ½ medium bunch (100 grams) spinach leaves (optional)
- ¼ medium bunch (50 grams) *bathua* leaves (optional)
- 2 tablespoons cornmeal (*makai ka atta*)
- 2 tablespoons oil
- 2 medium onions, finely chopped
- 6-8 garlic cloves, finely chopped
- 2 inches ginger, finely chopped
- 4-6 green chillies, roughly chopped
- 1 teaspoon red chilli powder
- 2 tablespoons butter
- Salt to taste

1. Clean, wash, drain and roughly chop mustard, spinach and *bathua* leaves.

2. Mix cornmeal with half a cup of water.

3. Heat oil in a pan; add chopped onions and sauté for two to three minutes or until translucent.

4. Add chopped garlic, ginger and green chillies and sauté for a few seconds. Add chilli powder and chopped mustard, spinach and *bathua* leaves. Stir in half a cup of water and cook over medium heat for ten minutes, stirring occasionally.

Desi Sabziyan

5 Mix in the cornmeal mixture and cook for five to six minutes more, stirring continuously.

6 Cool the mixture slightly and grind to a coarse paste. Reheat the mixture, add butter and salt to taste.

7 Stir well, and serve hot with *makai ki roti*.

CHEF'S TIP

Traditionally *Sarson ka Saag* is pounded to a paste with a wooden *mathni* or *ravai*, while it is being cooked. The process is quite cumbersome and time consuming, but the result is delicious.

Chane Aur Kathal Ki Sabzi *Desi Sabziyan*

Ingredients

1 cup Bengal gram (*chana*), soaked
500 grams jackfruit (*kathal*)
3 tablespoons oil
Salt to taste
½ teaspoon mustard seeds
1 sprig curry leaves
A pinch of asafoetida (*hing*)
1 tablespoon grated jaggery

Masala
1 teaspoon coriander seeds
½ teaspoon split black gram (*dhuli urad dal*)
¼ teaspoon fenugreek seeds (*methi dana*)
3-4 dried red chillies, broken in half
1 cup grated fresh coconut
1 tablespoon tamarind pulp

1 Soak *chana* in three cups of water for three or four hours. Drain.

2 Apply a little oil to your palms and the knife and remove the skin of the jackfruit; cut it into one-inch pieces. Mix in some salt and set aside for a few minutes.

3 Steam jackfruit for five minutes.

4 Pressure-cook soaked *chana* in two cups of water till pressure is released three times (three whistles), or till soft.

5 For the *masala*, heat one teaspoon of oil in a *kadai*. Add coriander seeds, *urad dal*

Desi Sabziyan

and fenugreek seeds. Sauté till lightly browned. Add red chillies and sauté for one minute. Grind with enough water, the coconut and tamarind pulp to a coarse paste.

6 Heat the remaining oil in a *kadai*. Add mustard seeds and curry leaves and sauté till the mustard seeds begin to splutter. Add asafoetida and the ground *masala*; stir well and cook for two minutes.

7 Stir in the boiled *chana*, steamed jackfruit, salt and jaggery.

8 Add half a cup of water and cook for five minutes over low heat stirring occasionally. Serve hot.

CHEF'S TIP

If a steamer is not available, boil jackfruit in one cup of water.

Kaalan

Desi Sabziyan

Ingredients

- 300 grams yam (*suran*)
- 2 unripe bananas
- 200 grams bottle gourd (*lauki/doodhi*)
- 10 green chillies
- 1 cup grated fresh coconut
- Salt to taste
- ½ teaspoon turmeric powder
- 2 cups yogurt, whisked
- 10-12 curry leaves
- 1 tablespoon coconut oil
- 1 teaspoon mustard seeds
- 2 dried red chillies

1 Peel and cut yam, bananas and bottle gourd into medium-sized fingers.

2 Grind green chillies with coconut to a smooth paste.

3 Boil one cup of water in a pan with a little salt and turmeric powder.

4 Add the vegetables and simmer till half-cooked. Stir in the whisked yogurt and stir well. Bring to a boil, lower heat and simmer.

5 With a flat perforated spoon skim the creamy layer that rises to the top and transfer to a bowl. Continue doing this till only the thin whey is left in the curry.

Desi Sabziyan

6 Add the curry leaves and salt to taste and cook till the liquid reduces by half.

7 Mix the coconut-chilli paste with the skimmed 'cream' and add to the vegetables. Cook for a couple of minutes and remove from heat.

8 In a small pan, heat coconut oil and add mustard seeds and red chillies. When the seeds begin to splutter, pour over the curry and cover immediately to trap the flavours. Serve hot.

CHEF'S TIP

Use thin buttermilk instead of water to cook the vegetables for a better flavour and aroma.

Dahi Baingan

Desi Sabziyan

Ingredients

- 6-8 medium-sized long brinjals
- 2 cups yogurt
- Salt to taste
- 2 tablespoons oil + for deep-frying
- ¼ teaspoon asafoetida (*hing*)
- 3-4 green cardamoms
- 1 tablespoon fennel (*saunf*) powder
- ½ tablespoon dried ginger powder (*sonth*)
- 2 teaspoons Kashmiri chilli powder

1 Wash and cut brinjals lengthways into quarters and soak in water till ready to use. Whisk yogurt and salt together.

2 Heat oil in a *kadai*. Drain brinjals, and pat them dry. Deep-fry till light brown and drain on absorbent paper.

3 Heat two tablespoons of oil in a pan; add asafoetida and green cardamoms. Sauté for a few seconds and immediately add the whisked yogurt. Stir in fennel, dried ginger and chilli powders.

4 Cook over medium heat for two to three minutes; add fried brinjals. Lower heat and cook, covered, for three to four minutes. Adjust seasoning and serve hot.

Arbi Ka Khatta Salan

Desi Sabziyan

Ingredients

- 20-25 (250 grams) colocasia (*arbi*)
- 2 tablespoons tamarind pulp
- Salt to taste
- ¾ inch ginger
- 7-8 garlic cloves
- 3 tablespoons peanuts (*moongphali*)
- 1 tablespoon sesame seeds (*til*)
- 3 tablespoons oil
- 1 teaspoon *paanch phoron* (page 15)
- 8-10 curry leaves
- 1 medium onion, sliced
- 2-3 green chillies, seeded and chopped
- ½ teaspoon turmeric powder
- 1 teaspoon red chilli powder
- 1 teaspoon coriander powder
- 1 teaspoon cumin powder
- A few sprigs of fresh coriander leaves, chopped

1. Boil *arbi* in four cups of salted water till tender. Peel and halve the larger *arbi* if necessary.

2. Grind ginger and garlic to a fine paste. Set aside.

3. Roast peanuts and sesame seeds separately till lightly browned. Cool and grind together with a little water to a fine paste.

4. Heat oil in a pan; add *paanch phoron* and sauté till the seeds begin to splutter. Add

curry leaves and sliced onion and sauté till golden brown. Add green chillies, ginger and garlic paste and sauté for a few minutes.

5 Add tamarind pulp, turmeric powder, chilli powder, coriander powder and cumin powder, and sauté for three to four minutes over low heat.

6 Add the peanut-sesame seed paste and sauté till the oil separates. Stir in two cups of water and simmer for about three to four minutes.

7 Add *arbi* and salt to taste. Simmer for another five minutes.

8 Sprinkle with chopped coriander leaves and serve hot with Hyderabadi or any other *paranthas*.

Malai Makai Palak

Desi Sabziyan

Ingredients

- ¼ cup fresh cream (*malai*)
- 1¼ cups sweetcorn kernels, boiled
- 3¼ medium bunches (650 grams) spinach
- 2½ tablespoons oil
- ½ teaspoon caraway seeds (*shahi jeera*)
- 2 large onions, chopped
- 1¼ teaspoons ginger paste
- 1¼ teaspoons garlic paste
- 4 green chillies, chopped
- Salt to taste
- 1¼ teaspoons dried mango powder (*amchur*)
- 1¼ tablespoons lemon juice
- 1¼ tablespoons dried fenugreek leaves (*kasoori methi*), roasted

1 Clean and wash spinach leaves thoroughly. Blanch in plenty of boiling water for one or two minutes; drain and refresh in ice-cold water. Purée in a blender.

2 Heat oil in a pan; add caraway seeds and sauté till they change colour. Add onions and cook till golden brown.

3 Add ginger and garlic pastes and sauté for a few seconds. Add green chillies and sauté for ten seconds.

Desi Sabziyan

4. Mix in the corn, *palak* purée, salt and *amchur* and cook for two minutes.

5. Add fresh cream and simmer till the gravy thickens. Remove from heat and stir in the lemon juice.

6. Sprinkle crushed *kasoori methi*, stir and serve immediately.

CHEF'S TIP

Refreshing spinach in ice-cold water after blanching helps to arrest the cooking and to retain its colour.

Khatta Meetha Kaddu

Desi Sabziyan

800 grams red pumpkin (*kaddu*)
4 tablespoons oil
¾ teaspoon fenugreek seeds (*methi dana*)
A large pinch of asafoetida (*hing*)
4 green chillies, chopped
Salt to taste
1 teaspoon turmeric powder
2 tablespoons coriander powder
2 inches ginger, cut into fine strips
2½ teaspoons red chilli powder
4 tablespoons sugar
3 tablespoons lemon juice
3 tablespoons fresh coriander leaves, chopped

1 Peel the pumpkin and cut into cubes.

2 Heat oil in a *kadai*. Add fenugreek seeds, asafoetida, green chillies and pumpkin and mix well.

3 Add salt, turmeric powder, coriander powder, ginger and red chilli powder and stir to mix. Add one-and-a-quarter cups of water, cover and cook over medium heat for ten to fifteen minutes.

4 Stir in the sugar, lemon juice and coriander leaves. Cover and cook over medium heat for ten minutes, or till pumpkin is very soft. Mash lightly and serve hot.

Simla Mirch Besan Ke Saath

Desi Sabziyan

Ingredients

- 4 medium green capsicums, cut into 1-inch cubes
- ¼ cup gram flour (*besan*)
- 2 tablespoons oil
- ½ teaspoon mustard seeds
- ½ teaspoon cumin seeds
- A pinch of asafoetida (*hing*)
- ¼ teaspoon turmeric powder
- Salt to taste
- 2 teaspoons red chilli powder
- ½ teaspoon *garam masala* powder
- 1½ teaspoons tamarind pulp
- ½ teaspoon sugar
- 2 tablespoons roasted peanuts, crushed

---

1 Heat oil in a pan; add mustard seeds and cumin seeds. When the mustard seeds begin to splutter and cumin seeds change colour, add asafoetida and *besan*. Stir continuously till light brown.

2 Add turmeric powder, salt, chilli powder and *garam masala* powder. Cook for one minute. Stir in approximately one cup of water to make a thick gravy.

3 Add tamarind pulp and sugar and mix well.

Desi Sabziyan

4 Add capsicums and stir well till coated with the *besan masala*; cover and cook over low heat till the capsicum is tender, stirring occasionally to prevent the *masala* from sticking to the bottom of the pan.

5 Sprinkle crushed peanuts and serve hot.

CHEF'S TIP

Choose capsicums which are unblemished, firm, glossy and heavy for their size. Quarter capsicums lengthways, remove and discard seeds and white membrane and cut into cubes.